Delightful & Frightful
Halloween
Recipes

Publications International, Ltd.
Favorite Brand Name Recipes at www.fbnr.com

Recipe Development: Recipes on pages 8, 10, 12, 16, 18, 20, 24, 26, 28, 32, 34, 38, 50, 54, 60 and 64 by Cynthia M. Colby.

Photography on pages 9, 11, 13, 17, 19, 21, 25, 27, 29, 33, 35, 39, 51, 55, 61 and 65 by Vincent Sanchez Photography.
Photographer: Vincent Sanchez
Prop Stylist: Kathy Lapin
Food Stylists: Moisette Sintov McNerney, Teri Rys-Maki

Pictured on the front cover *(clockwise from top left):* Pumpkin Patch Cut-Up Cake *(page 88),* Ghostly Delights *(page 44),* Haunted House *(page 70)* and Sweet Spiders *(page 50).*
Pictured on the back cover *(clockwise from top left):* Terrifying Tamale Pie *(page 10),* Graveyard Pudding Dessert *(page 80)* and Cobweb Cups *(page 54).*

ISBN: 1-4127-2080-X

Manufactured in China.

8 7 6 5 4 3 2 1

Microwave Cooking: Microwave ovens vary in wattage. Use the cooking times as guidelines and check for doneness before adding more time.

Preparation/Cooking Times: Preparation times are based on the approximate amount of time required to assemble the recipe before cooking, baking, chilling or serving. These times include preparation steps such as measuring, chopping and mixing. The fact that some preparations and cooking can be done simultaneously is taken into account. Preparation of optional ingredients and serving suggestions is not included.

Delightful & Frightful
Halloween
Recipes

Halloween Fun

Toasted Pumpkin Seeds

Preheat the oven to 350°F. Separate the pumpkin seeds from the fibers. Wash, drain and dry the seeds on paper towels. Coat 1½ cups seeds with 1 teaspoon vegetable oil.

Toss the seeds with salt (or omit salt and toss seeds with any of the suggested seasonings below) and spread them in a single layer on a baking sheet. Bake, stirring occasionally, 12 to 15 minutes or until golden brown.

Deviled Seeds: 1 tablespoon Worcestershire sauce and ¼ to ½ teaspoon chili powder

Sugar & Spice Seeds: 1 tablespoon sugar, ½ teaspoon ground cinnamon and ⅛ teaspoon ground allspice

Cheesy Seeds: 2 tablespoons grated Parmesan cheese and ½ teaspoon dried Italian seasoning

Ghostly Grog

With marshmallow ghosts, even hot chocolate can be spooky! Flatten large marshmallows and cut out Halloween shapes with miniature cookie cutters; place in a mug of hot chocolate and serve.

Spooky Spinning Game

For this game, make a spinner from a large circle of poster board. Divide the circle up into 16 even segments and write a dare, such as "Howl like a werewolf," or "Make 5 scary faces," in each segment. Cut out a spinner, such as a bat, from poster board. Punch a hole through the center

of the circle and through one end of the spinner; attach the spinner to the circle with a brass clasp, making sure the spinner can move freely. Have little goblins take turns spinning and performing their dare.

A Case of Fright

Pillow cases make great trick-or-treat bags! Start with white or orange pillow cases, and decorate them with fabric paints, felt cutouts and glitter. Have little monsters decorate the pillow cases to match their costumes, or with traditional Halloween colors and characters.

Haunted Tic-Tac-Toe

Cut out a 5-inch square from black construction paper or poster board. Glue four 5×1/8-inch green ribbons to the square to make a tic-tac-toe grid. Using 1 1/4-inch cookie cutters, trace 5 ghost shapes onto white construction paper and 5 pumpkin shapes onto orange construction paper. Cut out ghosts and pumpkins and decorate with a black marker.

Main Dish Mischief

Dem Bones

1 package (6 ounces) sliced ham
¾ cup shredded Swiss cheese
½ cup mayonnaise
1 tablespoon sweet pickle relish
½ teaspoon mustard
¼ teaspoon black pepper
6 slices white bread

1. Place ham in bowl of food processor or blender; process until ground. Combine ham, cheese, mayonnaise, relish, mustard and pepper in small bowl until well blended.

2. Cut out 12 bone shapes from bread using 3½-inch bone-shaped cookie cutter or sharp knife. Spread half of "bones" with 2 tablespoons ham mixture; top with remaining "bones." *Makes 6 sandwiches*

Terrifying Tamale Pie

   1 tablespoon vegetable oil
 ½ cup chopped onion
 ⅓ cup chopped red bell pepper
   1 clove garlic, minced
 ¾ pound ground turkey
 ¾ teaspoon chili powder
 ½ teaspoon dried oregano leaves
   1 can (14½ ounces) Mexican-style stewed tomatoes, undrained
   1 can (15 ounces) chili beans in mild chili sauce
   1 cup corn
 ¼ teaspoon black pepper
   1 package (8½ ounces) corn muffin mix plus ingredients to prepare mix
   2 cups taco-flavored shredded cheese, divided
     Bell peppers, pickle slices, pimiento pieces, onion, black olives and carrots for decoration

1. Heat oil in skillet over medium heat. Add onion and bell pepper; cook until crisp-tender. Stir in garlic. Add turkey; cook and stir until turkey is no longer pink. Stir in chili powder and oregano. Add tomatoes with liquid; cook and stir 2 minutes. Stir in beans with sauce, corn and pepper; simmer 10 minutes or until liquid is reduced by about half.

2. Preheat oven to 375°F. Grease 1½- to 2-quart casserole. Prepare corn muffin mix according to package directions; stir in ½ cup cheese. Spread half of turkey mixture in prepared casserole; sprinkle with ¾ cup cheese. Top with remaining turkey mixture and ¾ cup cheese. Top with corn muffin batter. Decorate with vegetables to make monster face. Bake 20 to 22 minutes or until golden.

Makes 6 to 8 servings

Terrifying Tamale Pie

Jack-O'-Lantern Chili Cups

2 cans (11.5 ounces each) refrigerated corn breadstick dough (8 breadsticks each) *or* 3 cans (4.5 ounces each) refrigerated buttermilk biscuits (6 biscuits each)
1 can (15 ounces) mild chili with beans
1 cup frozen corn
6 slices Cheddar cheese
    Olive slices, bell pepper and carrot pieces for decoration

1. Preheat oven to 425°F. Lightly grease 18 regular-size (2½-inch) muffin pan cups. Lightly roll out corn bread dough to press together perforations. Cut out 18 circles with 3-inch round cookie cutter. Press 1 circle onto bottom and 1 inch up side of each muffin cup.

2. Combine chili and corn in medium bowl. Fill each muffin cup with 1 tablespoon chili mixture. Cut out 18 circles from cheese with 2-inch round cookie cutter; place rounds over chili mixture in cups. Decorate cheese with olive, bell pepper and carrot pieces to resemble jack-o'-lanterns. Bake 10 to 12 minutes or until corn bread is completely baked and cheese is melted.

Makes about 8 servings

Jack-O'-Lantern Chili Cups

Mashed Potato Ghost

5 cups mashed Idaho Potatoes
    Waxed paper
½ cup small black olives

1. Cut ghost shape out of waxed paper to use as template.

2. Place template on serving dish or cookie sheet. Use rubber spatula to mold potatoes into ghost shape.

3. Slice olives to create circular shapes to be used for eyes and mouth.   *Makes 4 to 6 servings*

Note: To warm Mashed Potato Ghost, microwave on HIGH 3 to 5 minutes on microwavable plate. If using oven, place potatoes on cookie sheet and re-heat at 350°F, loosely covered with foil, 10 to 15 minutes or until heated through.

Favorite recipe from **Idaho Potato Commission**

For quick and spooky fun, cut out paper ghosts and bats and outline them with glow-in-the-dark markers. Hang them from the ceiling with black thread.

Ghoulish Punch

2 cups boiling water
1 package (8-serving size) *or* **2 packages (4-serving size) JELL-O® Brand Lime Flavor Gelatin Dessert**
2 cups cold orange juice
1 liter cold seltzer
   Ice cubes
1 pint (2 cups) orange sherbet, slightly softened
1 orange, thinly sliced
1 lime, thinly sliced

STIR boiling water into gelatin in large bowl at least 2 minutes until completely dissolved. Stir in cold juice. Cool to room temperature.

JUST before serving, pour gelatin mixture into punch bowl. Add cold seltzer and ice cubes. Place scoops of sherbet and fruit slices in punch. *Makes 10 servings*

Prep Time: 15 minutes

Monster Finger Sandwiches

**1 can (11 ounces) refrigerated breadstick dough
(12 breadsticks)
Mustard
12 slices deli ham, cut into ½-inch strips
4 slices Monterey Jack cheese, cut into ½-inch strips
1 egg yolk, lightly beaten
Assorted food colorings**

1. Preheat oven to 350°F. Place 6 breadsticks on ungreased baking sheets. Spread with mustard as desired. Divide ham strips evenly among breadsticks, placing over mustard. Repeat with cheese. Top with remaining 6 breadsticks. Gently stretch top dough over filling; press doughs together to seal.

2. Score knuckle and nail lines into each sandwich using sharp knife. Do not cut completely through dough. Tint egg yolk with food coloring as desired. Paint nail with egg yolk mixture.

3. Bake on lower oven rack 12 to 13 minutes or just until light golden. Let cool slightly. Serve warm or cool completely.

Makes 6 servings

Monster Finger Sandwiches

Quick Sand

¾ cup creamy peanut butter
5 ounces cream cheese, softened
1 jar (8 ounces or 1 cup) pineapple preserves
⅓ cup milk
1 teaspoon Worcestershire sauce
Dash hot pepper sauce (optional)
1 can (7 ounces) refrigerated breadstick dough
(6 breadsticks)
5 rich round crackers, crushed
Cut-up vegetables such as carrots, cucumber and
celery, or fruit such as apples and pears for dipping

1. Combine peanut butter and cream cheese in large bowl until well blended. Stir in preserves, milk, Worcestershire sauce and hot pepper sauce, if desired. Spread in 8- or 9-inch glass pie plate. Cover with plastic wrap and refrigerate until ready to serve.

2. Preheat oven to 375°F. Cut each breadstick in half crosswise; place on ungreased baking sheet. Make 3 slits in one short end of each breadstick half to resemble fingers. Cut small piece of dough from other short end; press dough piece into "hand" to resemble thumb. Bake 8 to 10 minutes or until golden brown.

3. Just before serving, sprinkle dip with cracker crumbs; serve with breadstick hands and vegetables and fruit. Garnish as desired.   *Makes 12 to 16 servings*

Quick Sand

Trick-or-Treat Pizza Biscuits

1 can (16 to 17 ounces or 8 biscuits) refrigerated
    jumbo biscuits*
3 tablespoons prepared pizza sauce
    Assorted pizza toppings such as cooked crumbled
        Italian sausage, pepperoni slices, sliced mushrooms
        and black olives
½ cup shredded pizza-blend or mozzarella cheese
1 egg yolk
1 teaspoon water
    Assorted food colorings

*Do not use butter-flavored biscuits.

1. Preheat oven to 375°F. Press 4 biscuits into 4-inch rounds
on ungreased baking sheet. Spread center of each biscuit
with about 2 teaspoons pizza sauce. Place desired pizza
toppings on each biscuit; top with 2 tablespoons cheese.
Press remaining 4 biscuits into 4-inch rounds and place
over cheese; press edges together to seal. Press design into
top of each biscuit with Halloween cookie cutter, being
careful not to cut all the way through top biscuit.

2. Combine egg yolk and water in small bowl. Divide yolk
mixture into several small bowls and tint each with food
colorings to desired colors. Decorate Halloween imprints
with egg yolk paints. Bake 12 to 15 minutes or until
biscuits are golden brown at edges.   *Makes 4 servings*

Trick-or-Treat Pizza Biscuits

Goblin's Brew

4 cups water
1 cup packed brown sugar
¾ cup granulated sugar
4 cinnamon sticks
¼ teaspoon whole cloves
4 cups fresh squeezed orange juice
3 cups apple cider
   Juice of 9 SUNKIST® lemons (1½ cups)
   Whole cloves
   Unpeeled lemon cartwheel slices

In large saucepan, combine water, sugars, cinnamon sticks and cloves. Bring to a boil, stirring to dissolve sugars. Reduce heat; simmer 5 minutes. Remove cinnamon sticks and cloves. Add orange juice, cider and lemon juice; heat. Garnish with clove-studded lemon cartwheels.

Makes 13 cups or 26 (½-cup) servings

For costumes, use face paint instead of masks. It's easier for little goblins to see when their view is not obstructed by a mask that doesn't fit.

Witches' Broomsticks

1 can (11 ounces) refrigerated French bread dough
1 egg yolk
1 teaspoon water
2 tablespoons grated Parmesan cheese
1 teaspoon dried oregano leaves
2 (12-inch) pieces black string licorice

1. Preheat oven to 350°F. Lightly grease baking sheet.

2. Cut bread dough into 8 equal pieces; roll each piece into 10-inch length. Fold top ⅓ of dough down, leaving 3 inches at bottom. Twist doubled top ⅔ portion to form broom handle. Cut bottom part into 5 or 6 lengthwise strips to form bristles of broom. Place shaped dough pieces, about 2 inches apart, on prepared baking sheet.

3. Beat together egg yolk and water with fork; brush evenly onto dough. Combine Parmesan cheese and oregano in small bowl; sprinkle evenly onto bottom portions of brooms.

4. Bake 15 to 20 minutes or until golden brown. Remove to wire rack; cool slightly.

5. Cut licorice evenly into 8 lengths; wrap around bottoms of brooms to "tie" bristles.   *Makes 8 servings*

Monster Mouth

1 teaspoon vegetable oil
1 medium onion, chopped
4 slices bacon, chopped
1 pound ground beef
2 medium plum tomatoes, seeded and chopped
½ teaspoon salt
¼ teaspoon black pepper
4 slices American cheese, chopped
½ package (12 ounces) jumbo pasta shells (about 18 shells), cooked and drained
Baby carrots, olives, red bell pepper, small pickles and cheese slices for decoration

1. Preheat oven to 350°F. Lightly grease 13×9-inch baking dish. Heat oil in large skillet over medium heat. Add onion and bacon; cook until onion is tender. Add beef; cook and stir about 5 minutes or until beef is no longer pink. Stir in tomatoes, salt and pepper. Stir chopped cheese into beef mixture. Spoon mixture into cooked shells; place in prepared baking dish.

2. Cut carrot into very thin strips. Cut small slit into olives; poke one end of thin carrot strips into olives for eyes. Cut red bell pepper into fang shapes. Slice pickle lengthwise into tongue shape. Cut cheese slice into zig-zag pattern for teeth.

3. Bake shells 3 to 5 minutes or until shells are hot; remove from oven. Decorate as desired with olive and carrot eyes, bell pepper fangs, pickle tongue and cheese teeth. Serve immediately.   *Makes about 6 servings*

Monster Mouth

Silly Snake Sandwich

½ **cup peanut butter**
1 **loaf (½ pound) sliced French or Italian bread, about**
     11 inches long and 3 inches wide
     Red bell pepper, black olive, green olive
½ **cup jelly, any flavor**
¼ **cup marshmallow creme**

1. Using small amount of peanut butter to attach, "glue" first 2 inches (3 to 4 slices) bread loaf together to make snake head. Cut bell pepper into 2-inch-long tongue shape. Make very small horizontal slice in heel of bread, being careful not to cut all the way through. Place "tongue" into slice. Cut black olive in half lengthwise; attach with peanut butter to snake head for eyes. Cut 2 small pieces from green olive; attach with peanut butter for nostrils. Set snake head aside.

2. Combine remaining peanut butter, jelly and marshmallow creme in small bowl until smooth. Spread on half of bread slices; top with remaining bread slices.

3. Place snake head on large serving tray. Arrange sandwiches in wavy pattern to resemble slithering snake. Serve immediately.   *Makes about 8 small sandwiches*

Silly Snake Sandwich

Spooky Sides & Snacks

Indian Corn

¼ cup butter or margarine
1 package (10.5 ounces) mini marshmallows
  Yellow food coloring
8 cups peanut butter and chocolate puffed corn cereal
1 cup candy-coated chocolate pieces, divided
10 lollipop sticks
  Tan and green raffia

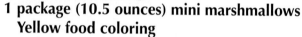

1. Line large baking sheet with waxed paper; set aside. Melt butter in large heavy saucepan over low heat. Add marshmallows; stir until melted and smooth. Tint with food coloring until desired shade is reached. Add cereal and ½ cup chocolate pieces; stir until evenly coated. Remove from heat.

continued on page 30

Indian Corn, continued

2. With lightly greased hands, quickly divide mixture into 10 oblong pieces. Push lollipop stick halfway into each oblong piece; shape like ear of corn. Place on prepared baking sheet; press remaining ½ cup chocolate pieces into each "ear." Let treats set.

3. Tie or tape raffia to lollipop sticks to resemble corn husks.   *Makes 10 servings*

Sticks 'n' Stones

   4 **cups caramel corn**
   4 **cups unseasoned croutons**
   ¾ **cup sesame sticks**
   ¾ **cup honey roasted peanuts**
   ¾ **cup toasted pumpkin or sunflower seeds***
   ¼ **cup butter, melted**
   1 **package (1 ounce) dry ranch-style salad dressing mix**
  10 **flat-bottomed ice cream cones**

*To toast seeds, place in single layer on baking sheet. Bake at 350°F for 7 to 10 minutes or until golden brown, stirring occasionally; cool.

1. Preheat oven to 300°F.

2. Combine caramel corn, croutons, sesame sticks, peanuts and toasted pumpkin seeds on ungreased jelly-roll pan. Drizzle with butter; sprinkle with dressing mix and toss to coat.

3. Bake 15 minutes, stirring occasionally. Cool 10 minutes on pan. Turn out onto paper towels; cool completely.

4. Tie cones with black and orange ribbons, if desired. Serve snack mix in cones.   *Makes 10 cups snack mix*

Pumpkin Maple Cream Cheese Muffins

   4 ounces cream cheese, softened
   ¾ cup plus 2 tablespoons packed brown sugar, divided
   3½ teaspoons maple flavoring, divided
   2 cups all-purpose flour
   ½ cup chopped walnuts
   2 teaspoons baking powder
   1 teaspoon ground cinnamon
   ½ teaspoon baking soda
   ¼ teaspoon salt
   1 cup LIBBY'S® Solid Pack Pumpkin
   ¾ cup CARNATION® Evaporated Milk
   2 eggs
   ¼ cup vegetable oil
   Nut Topping (recipe follows)

COMBINE cream cheese, 2 tablespoons brown sugar and 1½ teaspoons maple flavoring in small bowl until blended; set aside. Mix flour, ¾ cup brown sugar, walnuts, baking powder, cinnamon, baking soda and salt in large bowl. Combine pumpkin, evaporated milk, eggs, oil and remaining 2 teaspoons maple flavoring; mix well. Add pumpkin mixture to flour mixture, mixing just until blended.

SPOON into 12 greased or paper-lined muffin cups (cups will be very full). Dollop 1 heaping teaspoon of cream cheese mixture into center of each cup, pressing into batter slightly. Sprinkle Nut Topping over muffins.

BAKE in preheated 400°F. oven for 20 to 25 minutes or until wooden pick inserted in centers comes out clean. Cool in pan for 5 minutes; remove to wire rack to cool completely.   *Makes 12 muffins*

Nut Topping: COMBINE 2 tablespoons packed brown sugar and ¼ cup chopped walnuts in small bowl.

Shrunken Heads

4 small apples, such as Gala
  Lemon juice
3 tablespoons packed brown sugar
2 tablespoons butter, melted
¾ teaspoon ground cinnamon
⅛ teaspoon apple pie spice
  Dash salt
  Ice cream
  Caramel ice cream topping
  Colored sprinkles (optional)

1. Preheat oven to 400°F. Grease baking dish. Wash and core apples. Cut apples in half lengthwise; brush cut sides with lemon juice. Carve face on each apple half.

2. Combine brown sugar, melted butter, spices and salt in small bowl; brush over all sides of apples, filling face cutouts. Place apples, cut side down, in baking dish. Pour remaining brown sugar mixture over apples in dish. Bake 18 to 20 minutes or until apples are tender.

3. For each serving, place scoop of ice cream in bowl and drizzle with caramel topping. Top with apple half and sprinkles, if desired. *Makes 8 servings*

Shrunken Heads

Bubbling Cauldron

1 package (16 ounces) processed cheese with jalapeño peppers
2 cans (15 ounces each) black beans, well drained
1 cup medium or hot salsa
2 loaves (18 ounces each) round marble rye bread, unsliced
Pretzel rods and cocktail rye or pumpernickel bread

1. Melt cheese in medium saucepan over low heat, stirring occasionally. Remove from heat. Stir in beans and salsa. Carefully cut center out of bread, leaving 1½-inch shell. Cut bread center into pieces for dipping.

2. Reserve 1 pretzel rod. Arrange remaining pretzel rods on serving plate to resemble campfire logs. Place bread cauldron on pretzels; fill with cheese dip, allowing some to spill over top of bread cauldron. Arrange bread pieces and cocktail bread around cauldron. Place reserved pretzel rod in cheese dip; serve. *Makes 20 servings*

Use your favorite Halloween cookie cutters to cut scary shapes from the cocktail bread.

Bubbling Cauldron

Boo!! Brownies

6 squares (1 ounce each) semi-sweet chocolate,
   coarsely chopped
¼ cup (½ stick) plus 2 tablespoons butter, softened and
   divided
1 tablespoon freeze dried coffee granules
1 tablespoon boiling water
½ cup granulated sugar
2 large eggs
¾ cup all-purpose flour
½ teaspoon each baking powder and ground cinnamon
¼ teaspoon salt
1 cup "M&M's"® Chocolate Mini Baking Bits, divided
½ cup white frosting
   Assorted food colorings

Preheat oven to 350°F. Line 8×8×2-inch baking pan with aluminum foil, leaving 1½-inch overhang on two sides. Grease foil; set pan aside. In saucepan melt chocolate and 2 tablespoons butter over low heat stirring constantly. Remove from heat; cool. In bowl mix coffee granules and water; set aside. In large bowl beat ¼ cup butter, sugar and eggs; stir in chocolate mixture and coffee. In bowl mix flour, baking powder, cinnamon and salt; add to chocolate mixture. Stir in ½ cup "M&M's"® Chocolate Mini Baking Bits. Spread batter in prepared pan. Bake 30 to 35 minutes or until toothpick inserted in center comes out clean. Cool on wire rack. Lift brownies out of pan using foil. Cut into Halloween shapes using 3-inch cookie cutters. Tint frosting desired colors; spread over each brownie. Decorate with remaining ½ cup "M&M's"® Chocolate Mini Baking Bits.

Makes 8 to 10 brownies

Top to bottom: Boo!! Brownies and
"Here's Looking at You" Yummies (page 41)

Witches' Snack Hats

1 package (18 ounces) refrigerated sugar cookie dough
¼ cup unsweetened cocoa powder
1½ cups semisweet chocolate chips, divided
16 sugar ice cream cones
⅓ cup butter
3 cups dry cereal (mixture of puffed corn, bite-sized wheat and toasted oat cereal)
½ cup roasted pumpkin seeds
½ cup chopped dried cherries or raisins
1⅓ cups powdered sugar
Assorted colored sugars and decors

1. Preheat oven to 350°F. Grease cookie sheets; set aside. Remove dough from wrapper according to package directions. Combine dough and cocoa powder in large bowl; mix until well blended. Evenly divide dough into 16 pieces; shape into balls. Flatten each ball on prepared cookie sheet into 3½- to 4-inch circle. Bake 6 to 8 minutes or until set. Cool on cookie sheets 5 minutes; transfer to wire racks to cool completely.

2. Line large tray with waxed paper. Place 1 cup chocolate chips in small microwavable bowl. Microwave at HIGH 1 to 1½ minutes or until melted, stirring at 30-second intervals. Coat sugar cones with chocolate using clean pastry brush. Stand up on prepared tray; let set.

continued on page 40

Witches' Snack Hats

3. Place remaining ½ cup chocolate chips and butter in small microwavable bowl. Microwave at HIGH 1 to 1½ minutes or until melted, stirring at 30-second intervals. Stir mixture to blend well.

4. Place cereal, pumpkin seeds and cherries in large bowl. Pour chocolate mixture over cereal mixture and stir until thoroughly coated. Sprinkle mixture with powdered sugar, ⅓ cup at a time, carefully folding and mixing until thoroughly coated.

5. Fill cone with snack mix. Brush cone edge with melted chocolate; attach to center of cookie and let set. Repeat with remaining cones, snack mix and cookies. Decorate hats as desired with melted chocolate, colored sugars and decors. *Makes 16 servings*

To use these hats as place cards, simply write each guest's name on the hat with melted white chocolate, frosting or decorating gel.

"Here's Looking at You" Yummies

½ cup creamy or crunchy peanut butter
2 tablespoons butter, softened
¾ to 1 cup powdered sugar, divided
1¼ cups crisp rice cereal
1¼ cups "M&M's"® Semi-Sweet Chocolate Mini Baking
   Bits, divided
4 squares (2 ounces each) almond bark
   Red decorating gel

Line cookie sheet with waxed paper; set aside. In large bowl combine peanut butter and butter. Stir in ½ cup powdered sugar until well blended. Stir in cereal and 1 cup "M&M's"® Semi-Sweet Chocolate Mini Baking Bits. Stir in ¼ cup powdered sugar. If mixture is too sticky, stir in remaining ¼ cup powdered sugar. Shape dough into 1½-inch balls. Place on prepared cookie sheet. Refrigerate 1 hour. Line another cookie sheet with waxed paper; set aside. Melt almond bark according to package directions. Dip balls into almond bark, one at a time; gently shake off excess. Place treat on prepared cookie sheet. Decorate with remaining ¼ cup "M&M's"® Semi-Sweet Chocolate Mini Baking Bits and decorating gel to look like eyes. Store in tightly covered container.   *Makes 2 dozen treats*

Trick-or-Treat Ice Cream Sandwiches

½ **cup margarine, softened**
¾ **cup granulated sugar**
¾ **cup packed light brown sugar**
3 **egg whites**
1 **teaspoon vanilla**
2½ **cups all-purpose flour**
1½ **teaspoons baking soda**
1 **teaspoon ground cinnamon**
½ **teaspoon salt**
1 **package (6 ounces) semisweet chocolate chips**
1½ **cups ice cream or orange sherbet**

1. Preheat oven to 350°F. Spray baking sheets with nonstick cooking spray; set aside.

2. Beat margarine in large bowl until creamy. Add sugars; beat until fluffy. Blend in egg whites and vanilla. Combine flour, baking soda, cinnamon and salt in medium bowl. Add to margarine mixture; mix until well blended. Stir in chocolate chips.

3. Drop cookie dough by heaping teaspoonfuls onto prepared baking sheets, making 48 cookies. Bake until cookies are lightly browned, 10 to 12 minutes. Remove to wire racks to cool completely.

4. For each sandwich, place 1 tablespoon ice cream on flat side of 1 cookie; top with second cookie, flat side down. Press cookies together gently to even out ice cream layer. Repeat with remaining cookies and ice cream. Wrap tightly and store in freezer.

Makes 2 dozen sandwich cookies

Trick-or-Treat Ice Cream Sandwiches

Midnight Monster Munchies

Ghostly Delights

1 package (18 ounces) refrigerated cookie dough,
   any flavor
1 cup prepared vanilla frosting
¾ cup marshmallow creme
32 chocolate chips for decoration

1. Preheat oven to 350°F. Using about 1 tablespoon dough for body and about 1 teaspoon dough for head, form cookie dough into ghost shapes on greased cookie sheets. Bake 10 to 11 minutes or until browned. Cool 1 minute on cookie sheet; place warm cookies on serving plates.

2. While cookies are baking, combine frosting and marshmallow creme in small bowl until well blended.

3. Frost each ghost with frosting mixture. Press 2 chocolate chips, points up, into frosting mixture to make eyes on each ghost. Decorate with additional candy, if desired.

Makes 16 servings

Frost-on-the-Pumpkin Cookies

2 cups all-purpose flour
1 teaspoon baking powder
1 teaspoon ground cinnamon
½ teaspoon baking soda
½ teaspoon ground nutmeg
1 cup butter, softened
¾ cup JACK FROST® Granulated Sugar
¾ cup firmly packed JACK FROST® Brown Sugar
1 cup canned pumpkin
1 egg
2 teaspoons vanilla
½ cup raisins
½ cup chopped walnuts
Cream Cheese Frosting (recipe follows)

Preheat oven to 350°F. In small mixing bowl, combine flour, baking powder, cinnamon, baking soda and nutmeg. Set aside. In large mixer bowl, beat butter for 1 minute. Add granulated sugar and brown sugar; beat until fluffy. Add pumpkin, egg and vanilla; beat well. Add flour mixture to pumpkin mixture; mix until well blended. Stir in raisins and walnuts. Drop by teaspoonfuls 2 inches apart onto greased cookie sheet.

Bake 10 to 12 minutes. Cool on cookie sheet for 2 minutes. Transfer to wire rack; cool completely. Frost with Cream Cheese Frosting. Garnish with chopped nuts, if desired.   *Makes 48 cookies*

Cream Cheese Frosting: In medium mixing bowl, beat 3 ounces softened cream cheese, ¼ cup softened butter and 1 teaspoon vanilla until light and fluffy. Gradually add 2 cups JACK FROST® Powdered Sugar, beating until smooth.

Giant Candy Corn Cookies

  1 cup margarine or butter
²/₃ cup sugar
²/₃ cup light corn syrup
  1 teaspoon orange extract
  1 egg, beaten
  4 cups all-purpose flour
  2 teaspoons DAVIS® Baking Powder
¼ teaspoon yellow food coloring
¼ teaspoon red food coloring

1. Stir margarine, sugar and corn syrup in 3-quart saucepan over medium heat until margarine melts and sugar dissolves. Remove from heat; stir in orange extract. Cool 5 minutes; blend in egg.

2. Mix flour and baking powder in medium bowl; slowly blend in egg mixture to make a stiff dough. Shape ¼ of dough into 12×1½-inch log; set aside. Knead yellow food coloring into remaining dough on waxed paper; divide in half. Knead red food coloring into one piece of yellow dough on waxed paper to make orange. Shape both yellow and orange doughs into separate 12×2½-inch logs. Stack orange log over yellow log; top with plain log. Wrap; refrigerate several hours or until firm.

3. Let dough stand at room temperature 10 minutes. Cut stacked log into 24 (½-inch-thick) slices; place on lightly greased baking sheet. Flatten each piece, shaping into triangle about ⅛ inch thick.

4. Bake at 350°F 9 to 11 minutes until lightly brown. Do not overbake. Cool on wire rack; store in airtight container.

Makes 2 dozen cookies

Tombstone Brownies

1 package (21.5 ounces) brownie mix plus ingredients
    to prepare mix
1 cup chocolate fudge frosting
2 milk chocolate candy bars (1.55 ounces each)
    White icing
¾ cup flaked coconut, tinted green*
12 pumpkin candies

*To tint coconut, mix small amount of food coloring (paste or liquid) with
1 teaspoon water in bowl. Add coconut and stir until evenly coated.

1. Preheat oven to 350°F. Line 13×9-inch baking pan with
foil, extending foil beyond edges of pan; grease foil.

2. Prepare brownie mix according to package directions.
Spread in prepared pan. Bake 30 to 35 minutes. Do not
overbake. Cool in pan on wire rack.

3. Using foil as handles, remove brownies from pan; peel
off foil. Frost with chocolate frosting. Cut brownies into
twelve 4×2-inch bars.

4. Break chocolate bars into pieces along scored lines.
Using white icing, write "R.I.P." on chocolate pieces. Let
stand until set.

5. Press 1 chocolate piece into end of each brownie for
tombstone. Sprinkle tinted coconut on each brownie for
grass. Place 1 pumpkin candy on coconut.

Makes 12 servings

Tombstone Brownies

Sweet Spiders

1 package (18 ounces) refrigerated sugar cookie dough
¼ cup unsweetened cocoa powder
3 to 4 tablespoons seedless red raspberry or cherry preserves*
Chocolate licorice
Decors, cinnamon candies, assorted icings, sprinkles and mini chocolate chips

*If there are large pieces of fruit in preserves, purée in food processor until smooth.

1. Preheat oven to 350°F. Grease cookie sheets; set aside. Remove dough from wrapper. Combine dough and cocoa powder in large bowl; mix until well blended.

2. Evenly divide dough into 20 pieces. Shape each piece into 2 (1-inch) balls and 1 (½-inch) ball. For each spider body, flatten 1 (1-inch) ball into 2-inch circle on prepared cookie sheet. Place ½ teaspoon preserves in center of circle. Flatten remaining 1-inch ball into 2-inch circle and place over preserves, sealing dough edges. Cut licorice into 1½-inch pieces; cut pieces in half lengthwise. Press licorice into spider body for legs.

3. For each spider head, slightly flatten ½-inch ball and lightly press into spider body. Press decors or cinnamon candies into head for eyes.

4. Bake 10 to 12 minutes or until dough is set. Cool on cookie sheets 10 minutes; transfer to wire racks to cool completely. Decorate as desired with assorted icings, decors, sprinkles and mini chocolate chips.

Makes 20 cookies

Sweet Spiders

Boo-tiful Cupcakes

24 Reynolds® Halloween Bake Cups
1 package (about 18 ounces) cake mix
1 container (16 ounces) vanilla frosting
   Orange food color
   Halloween decorator sprinkles
1 cup premier white morsels
2 teaspoons shortening (not butter or margarine)
   Cut-Rite® Wax Paper

PREHEAT oven to 350°F. Place Reynolds Halloween Bake Cups in muffin pans; set aside. Prepare cake mix following package directions for 24 cupcakes. Spoon batter into bake cups. Bake as directed. Cool.

TINT frosting with orange food color; frost cupcakes. Sprinkle with Halloween decorator sprinkles.

MELT premier white morsels following package directions Add shortening; stir until melted. Spoon melted morsels into ghost shapes on cookie sheet lined with Cut-Rite Wax Paper. Use chocolate sprinkles for eyes. Refrigerate until firm. Stand one ghost in center of each cupcake.

Makes 24 cupcakes

Pumpkin Face Surprise Cookies

⅔ cup butter or margarine, softened
¾ cup sugar
1 egg
1 teaspoon vanilla extract
2 cups all-purpose flour
⅓ cup HERSHEY'S Cocoa
1½ teaspoons baking powder
1 tablespoon milk
1 HERSHEY'S SYMPHONY® Milk Chocolate Bar
  (7 ounces)
Orange decorating frosting

1. Beat butter, sugar, egg and vanilla in large bowl until fluffy. Stir together flour, cocoa and baking powder; add alternately with milk to butter mixture, beating well after each addition. Divide dough into quarters. Shape each quarter into ball; flatten slightly. Wrap individually in plastic wrap. Refrigerate dough 1 to 2 hours or until firm enough to handle. Meanwhile, break milk chocolate bar into pieces on scored lines; cut each piece in half.

2. Heat oven to 350°F.

3. Working with one portion of dough at a time on floured surface, roll to about ⅛-inch thickness. Using 2-inch round cookie cutter, cut dough into even number of rounds. Place half the rounds on ungreased cookie sheet. Place one chocolate piece in center of each round. Place remaining rounds on top. Using tines of fork, seal edges.

4. Bake 8 minutes or until set. Remove from cookie sheet to wire rack. Cool completely. With frosting, decorate tops of cookies to resemble pumpkin faces.

Makes about 40 cookies

Cobweb Cups

**1 package (19.8 ounces) brownie mix plus ingredients
   to prepare mix**
½ cup mini chocolate chips
2 ounces cream cheese, softened
1 egg
2 tablespoons sugar
2 tablespoons all-purpose flour
¼ teaspoon vanilla

1. Preheat oven to 350°F. Line 18 regular-size (2½-inch) muffin cups with paper muffin cup liners. Prepare brownie mix according to package directions for cakelike brownies. Stir in chocolate chips. Spoon batter into prepared muffin cups, dividing evenly.

2. Combine cream cheese and egg in small bowl; beat until well combined. Add sugar, flour and vanilla; beat until well combined.

3. Place cream cheese mixture in resealable plastic food storage bag; seal bag. With scissors, snip off small corner from one side of bag. Pipe cream cheese mixture in concentric circle design on each cupcake; draw toothpick through cream cheese mixture, out from center, 6 to 8 times.

4. Bake 20 to 25 minutes or until toothpick inserted into centers comes out clean. Cool in pans on wire racks 15 minutes. Remove to racks; cool completely.

Makes 18 cupcakes

Cobweb Cups

Monster Pops

1⅔ cups all-purpose flour
1 teaspoon baking soda
½ teaspoon salt
1 cup (2 sticks) butter or margarine, softened
¾ cup granulated sugar
¾ cup packed brown sugar
2 teaspoons vanilla extract
2 eggs
2 cups (12-ounce package) NESTLÉ® TOLL HOUSE®
  Semi-Sweet Chocolate Morsels
2 cups quick or old-fashioned oats
1 cup raisins
About 24 wooden craft sticks
1 container (16 ounces) prepared vanilla frosting,
  colored as desired, or colored icing in tubes

COMBINE flour, baking soda and salt in small bowl. Beat butter, granulated sugar, brown sugar and vanilla in large mixer bowl until creamy. Beat in eggs. Gradually beat in flour mixture. Stir in morsels, oats and raisins. Drop dough by level ¼-cup measure 3 inches apart onto ungreased baking sheets. Shape into round mounds. Insert wooden stick into side of each mound.

BAKE in preheated 325°F. oven for 14 to 18 minutes or until golden brown. Cool on baking sheet for 2 minutes; remove to wire racks to cool completely.

DRAW Halloween characters on pops using frosting and icing. *Makes about 2 dozen cookies*

Monster Pops

Festive Pumpkins and Striped Green Snakes

2½ cups all-purpose flour
1½ teaspoons baking powder
 1 teaspoon ground cinnamon
 ¾ teaspoon salt
 1 cup granulated sugar
 ½ cup vegetable oil
 2 eggs, beaten
 1 teaspoon vanilla

Pumpkin Decoration
 Green sprinkles
 3 ounces light or Neufchâtel cream cheese
 1 teaspoon vanilla
 1 cup powdered sugar
 Red and yellow food coloring
 Black licorice, cut into small triangles for eyes and
  thin long pieces for mouth

Snake Decoration
 Green food coloring
 Red cinnamon candies for eyes

Preheat oven to 350°F. Lightly grease baking sheet.

In small bowl mix flour, baking powder, cinnamon and salt. In medium bowl combine granulated sugar, oil, eggs and vanilla. Slowly add flour mixture and mix well forming stiff dough. If you want to make both cookies, divide dough into 2 balls.

To make pumpkins, shape dough into 2-inch circles and flatten. Add stems to tops. Cover stems with green sprinkles. Bake 8 to 10 minutes. Remove from baking sheet and let cool. To make frosting, mix cream cheese and vanilla.

Add powdered sugar and mix thoroughly until smooth. Add equal amounts red and yellow food coloring to make orange. Spread over cooled pumpkins. Make face with licorice.

To make snakes, add about 8 to 10 drops green food coloring to dough. Mix in. Coloring will not mix in evenly yielding striped snakes. Roll out dough 6 to 7 inches long and ¼ inch wide. Shape dough with two "S" curves. Place 2 red candies for eyes. Bake 8 to 10 minutes. Snakes will cook quickly; be careful not to overbake. Carefully remove from baking sheet and let cool.

Makes 16 pumpkin and 20 snake cookies

Favorite recipe from **The Sugar Association, Inc.**

Play "Batty Words" at your Halloween party! Before the event, cut out large bat shapes from white or colored paper. Write a list of spooky words, with the letters scrambled, on each bat. At the party, hand out the bats and have each guest try to unscramble as many words as they can.

Tombstones

¾ cup all-purpose flour
3 tablespoons sugar
2 tablespoons unsweetened cocoa powder
¼ teaspoon salt
1 cup water
½ cup butter, cut into pieces
4 eggs
1 package (4-serving size) instant vanilla or white
   chocolate pudding and pie filling mix
¾ cup cold milk
   Orange food coloring
1 container (8 ounces) frozen nondairy whipped
   topping, thawed
   Icings and Halloween decors

1. Combine flour, sugar, cocoa and salt in small bowl. Bring water and butter to a boil in large saucepan over high heat, stirring until butter is melted. Reduce heat to low; add flour mixture. Stir until mixture forms ball. Remove from heat. Add eggs, one at a time, mixing well after each addition until mixture is smooth.

2. Preheat oven to 375°F. Lightly grease baking sheet. Spoon about ¼ cup dough onto prepared baking sheet. With wet knife, form into tombstone shape, about 3½×2-inches. Repeat with remaining dough to form 10 tombstones, placing about 2 inches apart. Bake 25 to 30 minutes or until puffed and dry on top. Remove to wire racks; cool completely.

continued on page 62

Tombstones

3. Meanwhile, combine pudding mix and cold milk in medium bowl until smooth; stir in food coloring. Cover and refrigerate about 20 minutes or until set. Stir whipped topping into pudding until well blended. Cover and refrigerate about 20 minutes or until set.

4. With serrated knife, carefully cut each tombstone in half horizontally; remove soft interior, leaving hollow shell. Decorate top of each shell with icing and decors as desired. Just before serving, fill bottom shells evenly with pudding mixture; cover with top shells.

Makes 10 servings

Cool Spiders

24 baked cupcakes, paper liners removed
1 tub (8 ounces) COOL WHIP® Whipped Topping, thawed
Chocolate sprinkles
Black licorice pieces and small candies for garnish

FROST tops and sides of cupcakes with whipped topping. Decorate with chocolate sprinkles. Insert licorice pieces into tops of cupcakes to create "spider legs." Top with candies for "eyes."

Makes 24 servings

Variation: To create "lady bugs," stir a few drops of red food coloring into whipped topping. Frost cupcakes as directed. Decorate with chocolate chips.

Prep Time: 5 minutes

Ginger Pumpkin Face Cookies

1 cup PLANTERS® Pecan Halves, divided
1 cup 100% bran cereal
¼ cup light molasses
1 egg, beaten
1¼ cups all-purpose flour
1 teaspoon baking soda
1 teaspoon ground ginger
¼ teaspoon ground cloves
½ cup margarine or butter, softened
1 cup sugar, divided
Powdered Sugar Icing, recipe follows
Candy corn, melted chocolate and colored sprinkles

1. Set aside 36 pecan halves; finely chop remainder.

2. Mix bran cereal, molasses and egg in small bowl; let stand 5 minutes. Mix flour, baking soda and spices in another bowl; set aside.

3. Beat margarine and ¾ cup sugar in bowl with mixer at medium speed until creamy; blend in cereal mixture. Stir in flour mixture until blended. Stir in chopped pecans. Form into 1-inch balls; roll in remaining ¼ cup sugar.

4. Place 2 inches apart on lightly greased baking sheets. Flatten balls with bottom of glass. Insert 1 whole pecan into top edge of dough for stem. Bake at 375°F for 7 to 9 minutes. Let stand 1 minute before removing to cooling racks. Frost with Powdered Sugar Icing and decorate with candy corn, melted chocolate and colored sprinkles.

Makes about 3 dozen cookies

Powdered Sugar Icing: Combine 2 cups powdered sugar and 3 to 4 tablespoons milk until smooth. Tint with red and yellow food coloring to make orange tone.

Teeny Tiny Witches' Hats

1½ **cups all-purpose flour**
½ **teaspoon baking powder**
⅛ **teaspoon salt**
½ **cup butter, softened**
⅔ **cup powdered sugar**
1 **egg**
½ **teaspoon vanilla**
2 **squares (1 ounce each) semisweet chocolate, melted**
36 **milk chocolate candy kisses, unwrapped**

1. Preheat oven to 350°F. Lightly grease cookie sheets.

2. Combine flour, baking powder and salt in medium bowl. Combine butter and powdered sugar in large bowl; beat until well blended. Add egg and vanilla; beat until blended. Stir in melted chocolate until blended. Gradually stir in flour mixture until well blended.

3. Shape dough into 36 balls; place 2 inches apart on prepared cookie sheets. Flatten each ball to ¼-inch thickness; press chocolate candy into center. Bake 6 to 7 minutes or until cookies are set. Cool completely on wire rack.   *Makes 3 dozen cookies*

Teeny Tiny Witches' Hats

Jumbo Jack-O'-Lantern Brownie

¾ **cup (1½ sticks) butter or margarine, melted**
1½ **cups sugar**
1½ **teaspoons vanilla extract**
 3 **eggs**
¾ **cup all-purpose flour**
½ **cup HERSHEY'S Cocoa**
½ **teaspoon baking powder**
¼ **teaspoon salt**
 Orange Buttercream Frosting (recipe follows)
 Decorating icing or gel and assorted candies

1. Heat oven to 350°F. Line 12-inch pizza pan with foil; grease foil.

2. Stir together butter, sugar and vanilla in medium bowl. Add eggs; with spoon, beat well. Stir together flour, cocoa, baking powder and salt; gradually add to egg mixture, stirring until well blended. Spread batter into prepared pan.

3. Bake 20 to 22 minutes or until top springs back when touched lightly in center. Cool completely in pan on wire rack.

4. Remove brownie from pan; peel off foil. Prepare Orange Buttercream Frosting; spread over top of brownie. Garnish as desired with decorating icing and candies to resemble jack-o'-lantern face.   *Makes 12 to 15 servings*

Orange Buttercream Frosting

3 tablespoons butter or margarine, softened
2 cups powdered sugar
2 tablespoons milk
½ teaspoon vanilla extract
Red and yellow food colors

Beat butter in small bowl until creamy. Gradually add powdered sugar, milk and vanilla, beating until smooth and of spreading consistency. Add additional milk, 1 teaspoon at a time, if needed. Stir in food colors for desired orange color.

HAUNTED HINT

Here's how to make a spooky bean bag toss game: cut the top flaps off of a large box. Paint the outside of the box black. Place the box on its open end and paint a big white ghost on one side. Draw a large open mouth on the ghost and cut it out. Have party guests try to toss bean bags or rolled-up socks through the ghost's open mouth.

Pumpkin Harvest Bars

1¾ cups all-purpose flour
2 teaspoons baking powder
1 teaspoon grated orange peel
1 teaspoon ground cinnamon
½ teaspoon salt
½ teaspoon ground nutmeg
¼ teaspoon ground ginger
¼ teaspoon ground cloves
¾ cup sugar
½ cup MOTT'S® Natural Apple Sauce
½ cup solid-pack pumpkin
1 whole egg
1 egg white
2 tablespoons vegetable oil
½ cup raisins

1. Preheat oven to 350°F. Spray 13×9-inch baking pan with nonstick cooking spray.

2. In small bowl, combine flour, baking powder, orange peel, cinnamon, salt, nutmeg, ginger and cloves.

3. In large bowl, combine sugar, apple sauce, pumpkin, whole egg, egg white and oil.

4. Add flour mixture to apple sauce mixture; stir until well blended. Stir in raisins. Spread batter into prepared pan.

5. Bake 25 to 30 minutes or until toothpick inserted in center comes out clean. Cool on wire rack 15 minutes; cut into 16 bars.   *Makes 16 servings*

Pumpkin Harvest Bars

Desserts To Die For

Haunted House

1 cup (2 sticks) butter, softened
2 cups firmly packed light brown sugar
¾ cup light corn syrup
2 large eggs
5¼ cups all-purpose flour
2 teaspoons each baking soda and ground ginger
1 teaspoon ground allspice
½ teaspoon ground cinnamon
   Royal Icing (page 72) and Decorating Glaze (page 72)
   Assorted food colorings
2 cups "M&M's"® Chocolate Mini Baking Bits

In large bowl cream butter and sugar until light and fluffy; beat in corn syrup and eggs. In medium bowl combine flour, baking soda and spices; blend into creamed mixture.

continued on page 72

70

Wrap and refrigerate dough 2 to 3 hours. Preheat oven to 350°F. Grease cookie sheets. Working with ⅓ of dough at a time on floured surface, roll to ⅛-inch thickness. Cut out 2 (10×6-inch) rectangles and 2 shapes for each diagram; place on cookie sheets. Roll scraps to ⅛-inch-thickness; cut out with Halloween cookie cutters; place on cookie sheets. Bake 5 to 7 minutes or until lightly browned. Cool completely. Cover 12-inch square of cardboard with aluminum foil to use as house base. Spoon Royal Icing into resealable plastic bag; seal bag. Cut tiny corner off bag. Pipe icing on edges of all house pieces including bottom; "glue" together at seams and onto base. Let stand at least 1 hour or until icing is set, supporting walls with heavy glass. Tint Decorating Glaze with food colorings. Spread house and cookies with glaze; decorate with "M&M's"® Chocolate Mini Baking Bits.   *Makes 1 centerpiece*

Royal Icing: In large bowl beat 3 egg whites until foamy. Add 3 cups powdered sugar; beat until stiff.

Decorating Glaze: In bowl combine 4 cups powdered sugar and ¼ cup water until smooth. If necessary, add additional water, 1 teaspoon at a time, to make a pourable glaze.

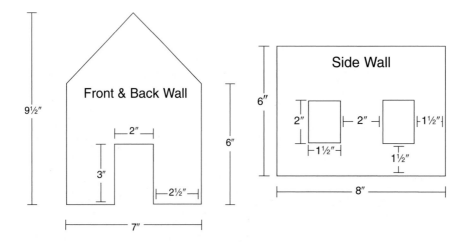

Friendly Ghost Puffs

  1 cup water
  ½ cup butter, cut into pieces
  1 cup all-purpose flour
  ¼ teaspoon salt
  4 eggs
  1 quart orange sherbet
    Powdered sugar
16 chocolate chips

1. Bring water and butter to a boil in medium saucepan over high heat, stirring until butter is melted. Reduce heat to low; stir in flour and salt until mixture forms a ball. Remove from heat. Add eggs, one at a time, beating after each addition until mixture is smooth.

2. Preheat oven to 400°F. Spoon about ⅓ cup dough onto ungreased baking sheet. With wet knife, form into ghost shape 3 inches wide and 4 inches long. Repeat with remaining dough to form ghosts, spacing them about 2 inches apart.

3. Bake 40 to 45 minutes or until puffed and golden. Remove to wire racks; cool completely.

4. Carefully cut each ghost in half horizontally; remove soft interior leaving hollow shell.

5. Just before serving, fill each shell bottom with about ½ cup orange sherbet. Cover with top of shell; sprinkle with powdered sugar. Position 2 chocolate chips on each ghost for eyes.

Makes 8 servings

Boo the Ghost

1 baked 13×9-inch cake, cooled
1 tub (8 ounces) COOL WHIP® Whipped Topping,
    thawed
2 chocolate wafer cookies
2 green candy wafers
    Candy corn
1 black jelly bean
    Black or red string licorice

CUT off 2 top corners of cake as shown in photo. Using small amount of whipped topping to hold pieces together, arrange cake pieces on serving tray as shown in photo.

FROST cake with remaining whipped topping. Decorate with cookies and candy wafers for eyes and candy corn for mouth. Make a spider using the jelly bean for its body and pieces of licorice for its legs. Store cake in refrigerator.

Makes 12 to 16 servings

HAUNTED HINT

Decorate your house with cute little pumpkin spiders! Paint faces on tiny pumpkins and glue on pipe cleaners for legs.

Top to bottom: Crazy Colored Halloween
Desserts (page 83) and Boo the Ghost

Webster's Web

1 (9-inch) round cake
2 cups Buttercream Frosting (recipe follows)
Blue food coloring
2 black licorice candies or jelly beans
1 black licorice whip, cut into 8 pieces

Supplies
Pastry bag and medium writing tip

Place cake on serving plate. Reserve ½ cup frosting; tint remaining 1½ cups frosting blue with food coloring. Frost cake with blue frosting. Using writing tip and white frosting, pipe 4 concentric circles, about 1 inch apart, and dot in the center of cake. Draw tip of knife through circles at regular intervals, alternating direction each time. Place candies for spider's body and head on cake. Place licorice pieces as spider legs.   *Makes 10 to 12 servings*

Buttercream Frosting

6 cups powdered sugar, sifted and divided
¾ cup butter or margarine, softened
¼ cup shortening
6 to 8 tablespoons milk, divided
1 teaspoon vanilla

Combine 3 cups powdered sugar, butter, shortening, 4 tablespoons milk and vanilla in bowl. Beat until smooth. Add remaining powdered sugar; beat until light and fluffy, adding more milk, 1 tablespoon at a time, as needed for good spreading consistency.   *Makes 3½ cups frosting*

Webster's Web

Caramel-Marshmallow Apples

1 package (14 ounces) caramels
1 cup miniature marshmallows
1 tablespoon water
5 or 6 small apples

1. Line baking sheet with buttered waxed paper; set aside.

2. Combine caramels, marshmallows and water in medium saucepan. Cook over medium heat, stirring constantly, until caramels melt. Cool slightly while preparing apples.

3. Rinse and thoroughly dry apples. Insert flat sticks in stem ends of apples.

4. Dip each apple in caramel mixture, coating apples. Remove excess caramel mixture by scraping apple bottoms across rim of saucepan. Place on prepared baking sheet. Refrigerate until firm.   *Makes 5 or 6 apples*

Caramel-Nut Apples: Roll coated apples in chopped nuts before refrigerating.

Caramel-Chocolate Apples: Drizzle melted milk chocolate over coated apples before refrigerating.

Top to bottom: Caramel-Nut Apple,
Caramel-Marshmallow Apple and
Caramel-Chocolate Apple

Graveyard Pudding Dessert

3½ cups cold milk
2 packages (4-serving size) JELL-O® Chocolate Flavor Instant Pudding & Pie Filling
1 tub (12 ounces) COOL WHIP® Whipped Topping, thawed
1 package (16 ounces) chocolate sandwich cookies, crushed
Decorations: assorted rectangular-shaped sandwich cookies, decorator icings, candy corn and pumpkins

POUR milk into large bowl. Add pudding mixes. Beat with wire whisk or electric mixer on lowest speed 2 minutes or until blended. Gently stir in whipped topping and ½ of the crushed cookies. Spoon into 13×9-inch dish. Sprinkle with remaining crushed cookies.

REFRIGERATE 1 hour or until ready to serve. Decorate rectangular-shaped sandwich cookies with icings to make "tombstones." Stand tombstones on top of dessert with candies to resemble a graveyard.　　*Makes 15 servings*

Prep Time: 15 minutes
Chill Time: 1 hour

Graveyard Pudding Dessert

Chocolate and Pumpkin Squares

½ cup (1 stick) butter or margarine, softened
1 cup sugar
2 eggs
1½ teaspoons vanilla extract
1½ cups all-purpose flour
1 teaspoon baking powder
½ teaspoon baking soda
¼ teaspoon salt
¼ cup HERSHEY'S Cocoa
½ cup canned pumpkin
½ teaspoon pumpkin pie spice
Chocolate Frosting (recipe follows)

1. Heat oven to 350°F. Grease 9-inch square baking pan.

2. Beat butter and sugar in medium bowl until well blended. Add eggs and vanilla; beat until smooth and creamy. Stir together flour, baking powder, baking soda and salt; gradually add to butter mixture. Remove 1¼ cups batter to small bowl; add cocoa, blending well. To remaining batter, blend in pumpkin and pumpkin pie spice. Spread chocolate batter into prepared pan; spread pumpkin batter over chocolate.

3. Bake 30 minutes or until brownies begin to pull away from sides of pan. Cool completely in pan on wire rack. Frost with Chocolate Frosting. Cut into squares.

Makes about 16 squares

Chocolate Frosting

    1 cup powdered sugar
 ¼ cup HERSHEY'S Cocoa
    3 tablespoons butter or margarine, softened
    2 to 3 tablespoons milk
 ½ teaspoon vanilla extract

Stir together powdered sugar and cocoa. Beat butter in small bowl until creamy; gradually add sugar mixture alternately with milk, beating until desired consistency. Stir in vanilla.   *Makes about 1 cup frosting*

Crazy Colored Halloween Desserts

    1 package (8 ounces) PHILADELPHIA® Cream Cheese, softened
    4 scoops KOOL-AID® Sugar-Sweetened Soft Drink Mix, any green or orange flavor
 ½ cup milk
    1 tub (8 ounces) COOL WHIP® Whipped Topping, thawed
 12 sponge cake dessert shells
    Assorted candies and cookies

BEAT cream cheese and soft drink mix in large bowl until well blended. Gradually beat in milk until smooth. Gently stir in whipped topping.

SPOON about ⅓ cup whipped topping mixture into each dessert shell. Decorate with candies and cookies to resemble pumpkins, spiders and witches. Refrigerate until ready to serve.   *Makes 12 servings*

A Little Country Pumpkin Cake

Cake
- 2 cups boiling water
- ½ cup raisins
- 2 cups granulated sugar
- 1 CRISCO® Stick or 1 cup CRISCO® all-vegetable shortening, melted, plus additional for greasing
- 1 can (16 ounces) solid-pack pumpkin (not pie filling)
- 4 eggs
- 2 cups all-purpose flour
- 1 tablespoon ground cinnamon
- 2 teaspoons baking powder
- 1 teaspoon baking soda
- 1 teaspoon ground ginger
- ¾ teaspoon salt
- ¼ teaspoon ground cloves

Frosting
- ¼ Butter Flavor CRISCO® Stick or ¼ cup Butter Flavor CRISCO® all-vegetable shortening
- 2 cups confectioners' sugar
- 3 tablespoons milk
- 1 teaspoon vanilla
- Chopped nuts

1. Heat oven to 350°F. Grease 10-inch round cake pan. Flour lightly. Place cooling rack on counter top for cooling cake.

2. For cake, pour boiling water over raisins in colander. Drain. Press lightly to remove excess water.

continued on page 86

A Little Country Pumpkin Cake

3. Combine granulated sugar, 1 cup melted shortening, pumpkin and eggs in large bowl. Beat at medium-high speed of electric mixer 5 minutes. Combine flour, cinnamon, baking powder, baking soda, ginger, salt and cloves in medium bowl. Add to pumpkin mixture, 1 cup at a time, beating at low speed after each addition until blended. Stir in raisins with spoon. Pour into pan.

4. Bake at 350°F for 55 to 60 minutes or until toothpick inserted in center comes out clean. DO NOT OVERBAKE. Remove cake to rack to cool. Cool 10 to 15 minutes before removing from pan. Place cake, top side up, on wire rack. Cool completely. Place cake on serving plate.

5. For frosting, melt ¼ cup shortening in small saucepan on low heat. Transfer to medium bowl. Add confectioners' sugar. Beat at low, then high speed until blended. Add milk and vanilla. Beat at high speed until smooth and frosting is of desired spreading consistency. Frost top and side of cake. Press nuts into side of cake and around outside top edge.

Makes 1 (10-inch) round cake (10 to 12 servings)

For a pretty table decoration, put tea lights in hollowed-out mini pumpkins or apples.

Huge Scary Spiders

2 ounces unsweetened chocolate
1¼ cups all-purpose flour
1½ teaspoons baking powder
¼ teaspoon salt
¼ cup margarine
1 cup sugar
1 egg, beaten
1 teaspoon vanilla
Red cinnamon candies

Preheat oven to 375°F. Lightly grease baking sheet.

In saucepan, melt chocolate over low heat. Let cool. In small bowl mix flour, baking powder and salt. In medium bowl, beat margarine on low speed until smooth. Add sugar and beat until creamy. Stir in egg, vanilla and chocolate. Add flour mixture and mix well forming stiff dough.

To make spider, shape 2-inch flat oval for body. Make spider's head by flattening a circle about ½ inch wide. Shape dough for 8 legs each about 2 inches long and less than ¼ inch wide. Attach head and legs to body. Put two red candies into head for eyes. Bake 5 to 8 minutes. Let spiders cool on baking sheet to avoid breaking when removing.   *Makes 20 cookies*

Favorite recipe from **The Sugar Association, Inc.**

Pumpkin Patch Cut-Up Cake

4 cups BAKER'S® ANGEL FLAKE® Coconut
Red and yellow food colorings
3½ cups Vanilla Buttercream Frosting (page 90), divided
Green food coloring
1 flat-bottom ice cream cone (for stem)
2 baked fluted tube cakes (12-cup), cooled
1 cup Chocolate-Coated Coconut (page 90)

TINT coconut orange using red and yellow food colorings.

TINT ½ cup of the frosting with green food coloring. Frost outside of ice cream cone with about ¼ cup of the green frosting; set aside. Reserve remaining ¼ cup green frosting.

USING small amount of plain frosting to hold pieces together, stack two cakes, flat sides together, on serving tray as shown in photograph. (If desired, insert bamboo skewers into cake layers to hold the cakes together.)

FROST cakes with remaining plain frosting; sprinkle with orange coconut. Invert ice cream cone in hole on top to form "stem." Pipe reserved green frosting on pumpkin to form lines using a pastry bag fitted with a small plain tip. Arrange Chocolate-Coated Coconut around base of pumpkin to resemble dirt.   *Makes 24 servings*

continued on page 90

Pumpkin Patch Cut-Up Cake

Vanilla Buttercream Frosting

1 package (16 ounces) powdered sugar
½ cup (1 stick) butter *or* margarine, softened
3 tablespoons milk
2 teaspoons vanilla

BEAT sugar, butter, milk and vanilla with electric mixer on low speed until well blended and smooth. If frosting becomes too thick, beat in additional milk by teaspoonfuls until of spreading consistency.

Makes about 2½ cups frosting

Chocolate-Coated Coconut: Microwave 2 squares BAKER'S® Semi-Sweet Chocolate in microwavable bowl on HIGH 1 to 2 minutes until almost melted, stirring every 30 seconds. Stir until completely melted. Add 1⅓ cups BAKER'S® Angel Flake® Coconut; mix well. Spread on cookie sheet, separating flakes with fork. Chill until set. Store in tightly covered jar. Makes 1½ cups coconut.

HAUNTED HINT

If goblins and ghouls are too young to help carve pumpkins, have them paint or decorate the pumpkins with markers, stickers and glitter.

Acknowledgments

The publisher would like to thank the companies and organizations listed below for the use of their recipes and photographs in this publication.

DAVIS® Baking Powder

Hershey Foods Corporation

Idaho Potato Commission

Kraft Foods Holdings

©Mars, Inc. 2002

Mott's® is a registered trademark of Mott's, Inc.

Nestlé USA, Inc.

PLANTERS® Nuts

The Procter & Gamble Company

REFINED SUGARS, INC.

Reynolds Metals Company

The Sugar Association, Inc.

Sunkist Growers

Index

Index